GETTING TO KNOW THE WORLD'S GREATEST ARTISTS

PICASSO

WRITTEN AND ILLUSTRATED BY MIKE VENEZIA

FRANKLIN WATTS

LONDON / NEW YORK / SYDNEY / TORONTO

To Pat and Gene with love

The author wishes to express a special thanks
to Sarah Mollman

Cover: Boy in Sailor Suit with Butterfly Net. 1938. Phototheque, SPADEM/Art Resource

First published in Great Britain 1989 by
Franklin Watts
96 Leonard Street
London, EC2

ISBN: 086313 978 7

Copyright © 1983 by Regensteiner Publishing Enterprises, Inc.

Printed in the United States of America.

Pablo Picasso was one of the greatest artists of the twentieth century. He was born in Malaga, Spain, in 1881, and died in France in 1973.

Picasso's father was an art teacher
at the local school. He encouraged his

son to paint and draw. He wanted
Picasso to become a great artist one
day.

The Altar Boy. 1896. Canvas.
Spain, Courtesy Abadia de Montserrat, Barcelona

Picasso's painting style changed many times during the period of his life. He was always trying new and different things.

The painting above was done when he was only fifteen years old.

Boy in Sailor Suit with Butterfly Net. 1938.
Phototheque, SPADEM/Art Resource

This painting was done when
Picasso was fifty-seven.

There's quite a difference between
the two paintings, isn't there?

Girl Before a Mirror. 1932. Canvas, 162.3 x 130.2 cm. New York, The Museum of Modern Art

Sometimes Picasso painted things that look very flat.

Bather with a Beach Ball. 1932. Canvas, 146.2 x 114.6 cm.
New York, The Museum of Modern Art

Sometimes he painted things that look so round you feel you could pick them out of the painting.

When Picasso was nineteen, he left Spain and went to Paris, France. Some of the first paintings he did there look a little bit like the work of other famous French artists.

This painting reminds many people or the work done by Toulouse-Lautrec. Some of Picasso's other early paintings remind people of the styles of Van Gogh, Gauguin, and Monet.

Le Moulin de la Galette. 1900. Canvas, 90 x 2 x 117 cm. New York, Solomon R. Guggenheim Museum

THE BLUE PERIOD

Then something happened!
Picasso's paintings changed. His work
became different from anyone else's

His best friend died, and Picasso felt
alone and sad. No one was buying his
paintings, and he was almost starving
to death.

Because of his mood, Picasso began
to paint with lots of blue (blue can be
a very sad colour). He made all the
people in his paintings look lonely
and sad.

The Old Guitarist. 1903. Panel, 122.9 x 82.6 cm. The Art Institute of Chicago

People argued about Picasso's blue paintings. Some thought they were great. Others (including Picasso's father) thought they were just too strange.

THE ROSE PERIOD

Picasso's Blue Period ended when
he met a girl called Fernande.
Fernande and Picasso fell in love and
soon a happier colour started
appearing in Picasso's paintings. This
was the beginning of the Rose Period.

Family of Saltimbanques. 1905. Canvas, 212.8 x 229.6 cm. Washington, D.C., National Gallery of Art

Not only were Picasso's colours happier during the Rose Period, but he started painting happier things, too. He met and painted a lot of circus people during this time. He often painted them with their animals.

The Rose Period didn't last very long, though, because Picasso found a new way to paint that was really exciting and different.

Portrait of D. H. Kahnweiler. 1910. Canvas, 100.6 x 72.8 cm. The Art Institute of Chicago

CUBISM

Cubism was the next style of painting that Picasso developed and made famous.

This is a cubist painting of one of Picasso's friends. The man in the painting looks like he's been broken up into little cubes. That's where the name cubism came from.

Look closely. Can you see the man's face, what he was wearing, his hands, a bottle, a glass, and perhaps his pet cat? Can you find anything else?

Cubism is one of the most important periods in the history of modern art.

For hundred of years, artists had tried very hard to paint things in such a way that they looked real. Then Picasso came along and started to

paint people and things that didn't
look the way they were supposed to.

Picasso was always shocking
people, but when he started painting
people who had eyes and noses in the
wrong places – well, even some of his
closest friends thought he had gone
too far.

Picasso kept working with cubism and changed it over the years. It became much more colourful and flatter looking. It also became easier to see what Picasso was painting.

In the painting *Three Musicians*, you can see the three musicians, and tell what instruments they're playing.

In another style that Picasso used for a while, he returned to painting people in a more realistic way.

Three Musicians. 1921. Canvas, 200.7 x 222.9 cm. New York, The Museum of Modern Art

Three Women at the Spring. 1921. Canvas, 203.9 x 174 cm.
New York, The Museum of Modern Art

Picasso had just visited Rome, a city filled with statues and monuments. When he returned from his trip, he did a series of paintings in which people look as if they've been chiselled out of stone, like statues.

GUERNICA

In 1937 something happened that made Picasso paint his most powerful and serious painting.

During a civil war that was going on in Spain, the small town of Guernica was destroyed by bombs. Thousands of innocent people were killed and injured.

Picasso became very angry and used all his skills to make a painting that would show the world how foolish war was. He named the painting Guernica, after the town.

Guernica. 1937. Canvas, 351 x 782 cm. Madrid, Museo del Prado

Picasso used dark colours, cubism,
and lots of expression to get his angry
feelings across in this painting.

He also used size. This painting is huge. It's almost four metres high and over seven metres wide!

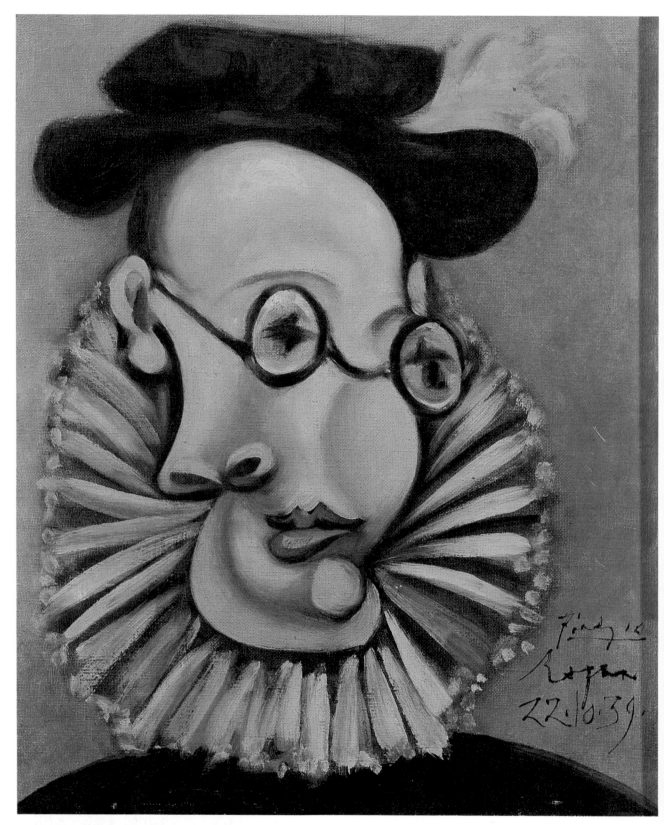

Portrait of Jaime Sabartés as a Spanish Grandee. 1939. Canvas, 46 x 38 cm. Spain, Picasso Museum

Many of Picasso's paintings look odd because of the way he moves eyes, noses, and chins around. But the amazing thing about these paintings is that the people in them can be easily recognised.

Look at the painting of Picasso's best friend, Jaime Sabartés, on the opposite page. Does it look like the same man shown in the painting below?

Jaime Sabartés, painted by Steve Dobson from a photograph by Gilberte Brassai

What made Picasso such a great artist was his originality. He had the imagination to try new and different things throughout his entire life.

The ape and her young. 1952.
Sculpture. Paris, Musee Picasso.
Gilraudon/Art Resource

The Old Fisherman. 1895.
Canvas, 82 x 62 cm. Courtesy Abadia
de Montserrat, Barcelona

Minotauromachia. 1935.
Etching, 49.2 x 69 cm.
The Art Institute of Chicago

Four Children Viewing a Monster.
1933. Etching, 33.5 x 44.8 cm
The Art Institute of Chicago

Weeping Woman. 1937.
Canvas, 60 x 49 cm. London,
The Bridgeman Art Library/Art Resouce

Picasso lived to be ninety-two years old. He was a great painter, but he was great at other things, too.

He made sculptures, prints and drawings, as well as beautiful coloured dishes and bowls. He even made costumes and scenery for ballets.

FACTS ABOUT PICASSO

When Picasso was born, the nurse thought he was dead. She left him on a table while she tried to comfort his mother. But Picasso's uncle, Don Salvador, who had been present at the birth and was himself a qualified doctor, realised that the nurse had made a terrible mistake. He is said to have blown cigar smoke into Picasso's face, to make him cry!

By the time he was 13, Picasso was a better painter than his father. One day, his father asked him to complete a painting by drawing in some pigeons' feet. When he saw how well the feet were drawn, Picasso's father handed over his brushes and paint to his son and said that he would never paint again.

When the family moved to Barcelona, Picasso applied to join the advanced art class at the city's School of Fine Arts. He was asked to do a number of drawings as an exam. He was given a month in which to complete the drawings, but Picasso handed them in after only one day!

In 1896, while he was still living in Barcelona, Picasso's first large oil painting, "The First Communion", was shown in what was then the most Important art exhibition ever held in the city. The following year, his second large oil painting, "Science and Charity", was given an honourable mention in the National Exhibition of Fine Art in Madrid and awarded a gold medal in a competition at Malaga. Picasso was still only 16!

In February 1901, the painter Carlos Casagemas, Picasso's friend from Barcelona, shot himself in a cafe in Paris after the girl he loved told him that she didn't love him. Picasso was very upset, and his painting, "The Burial of Casagemas", finished in the summer of that year, marked the start of his Blue Period.

In 1904, Picasso finally settled in Paris. He moved into an artist's studio called "Bateau-Lavoir", meaning "Laundry-boat", in Montmartre, the artists' quarter of the city. His girlfriend, Fernande Olivier, came to live with him. They had very little money, and Picasso sometimes had to paint by candlelight, when they could not afford to buy oil to light the lamps.

In 1907, Picasso painted a picture called "Les Demoiselles d'Avignon". It shows five naked women whose limbs are held at strange angles, and whose bodies look ugly and deformed. Two of the women's faces are like painted masks. Picasso's friends were shocked when they saw the painting. Some thought he had painted it as a joke. Others thought he was going mad. So Picasso rolled up the canvas and put it away. Years later, it was considered a masterpiece, and sold for a great deal of money. It is now seen as marking the start of Picasso's Cubist Period.

Picasso was always good at drawing portraits. Often while he was sitting at a café table, he would amuse himself by drawing, *upside-down*, a picture of the friend who was sitting opposite!

Picasso hardly ever gave his paintings titles, although he did date each work carefully. The titles which are used were mostly suggested by friends, or by the people cataloguing the paintings for an exhibition.

Picasso found it hard to think of a painting as being finished. He liked to keep paintings in his studio for months, even years, so that he could change them or add to them if he wanted to.

Picasso was married twice, and had many girlfriends. He had four children: the first, Paul, by his wife, Olga; the second, a daughter called Maia, by a girlfriend, Marie-Thérèse Walter; the third, Claude, and the fourth, Paloma, by another girlfriend, Françoise Gilot.

By 1945, Picasso was so famous that the sale of only one painting gave him enough money to buy a new house!

When someone dies, their family usually has to pay taxes called death duties to the government. Instead of money, Picasso's family gave the French government a large number of paintings from Picasso's private collection. These works are now in the Musée Picasso in Paris, which opened in 1985 with 203 paintings, 191 sculptures, 85 ceramics and over 3,000 drawings and sketches.

Picasso loved junk, and had huge collections of rocks, stones, fossils, bones, toys, masks, ornaments, postcards and other items. Many of these junk materials were used for his collage pictures and for his sculptures. One sculpture, "Goat", was made from a wicker basket (the belly), a palm branch (the spine and ribs), scrap iron (the shoulders), and clay pots (the udders). He created a bull's head out of an old bicycle saddle and handlebars, and in his sculpture, "Baboon with Young" (page 30), the baboon's head is made from a toy motor car.

Between 1916 and 1925, Picasso designed exciting, colourful costumes and sets for several ballets performed by the Russian ballet company, Ballets Russes. It was during his work on the first of these ballets, "Parade", that he met his first wife, the ballerina Olga Koklova.

TIME CHART

25 October 1881	Picasso is born in Malaga, Spain
1895	Enrols in the School of Fine Arts, Barcelona
1897	Passes the entrance exam to the Royal Academy of San Fernando in Madrid, but catches scarlet fever and spends over a year recovering
1899	Returns to Barcelona. Meets Carlos Casagemas and Jaime Sabartés
1900	Picasso and Casagemas move to Paris and open a studio in Montmartre
1901	Casagemas kills himself. Picasso returns to Madrid, then moves back to Paris. The Blue Period of his work begins
1902 – 1904	Picasso spends time in Barcelona and in Paris, finally settling in Paris. Meets Fernande Olivier, his girlfriend for the next seven years
1905	The Rose Period of his work begins
1909	Picasso's work enters its Cubist Period
1917	Meets the Russian dancer Olga Koklova
12 July 1918	Picasso and Olga marry
1927	Picasso meets a new girlfriend, Marie-Thérèse Walter
26 April 1937	The Germans bomb the town of Guernica. Picasso paints his famous mural
1939	Picasso's mother dies. The Second World War begins, and Picasso moves out of Paris to Royan, near Bordeaux
1940	Returns to Paris
1943	Meets new girlfriend, Françoise Gilot
1946	Picasso and Françoise move to the south of France
1948	Picasso attends the first World Peace Conference, in Warsaw, Poland
1949	Picasso creates a dove symbol for the second Peace Conference, in Paris
1950	Picasso receives the Lenin Peace Prize
1953	Meets Jacqueline Roque, who is to become his second wife
1962	Picasso receives the Lenin Peace Prize for the second time
8 April 1973	Picasso dies and is buried two days later at Chateau Vauvenargues, near Aix-en-Provence

WHERE TO SEE PICCASO'S WORK

Here is a list of some of the art galleries and museums in Britain and Europe where you can see some of Picasso's best-known paintings.

THE TATE GALLERY, LONDON, ENGLAND
Girl in a Chemise
Seated Nude
The Three Dancers

MUSÉE D'ART MODERNE DE LA VILLE DE PARIS, PARIS, FRANCE
The Burial of Casagemas
Les Trois Hollandaises

MUSÉE PICASSO, PARIS, FRANCE
Women Running on the Beach
The Pipes of Pan
Paul as Harlequin
Portrait of Dora Maar

MUSEO PICASSO, BARCELONA, SPAIN
The First Communion
Portrait of Jaime Sabartés (1939)

MUSEO DEL PRADO, MADRID, SPAIN
Guernica

STAATSGALERIE, STUTTGART, WEST GERMANY
Tumblers (Mother and Son)

STEDELIJK MUSEUM, AMSTERDAM, HOLLAND
Woman in a Fish Hat

NATIONAL GALLERY, PRAGUE, CZECHOSLOVAKIA
Self-Portrait (1907)

THE HERMITAGE, LENINGRAD, RUSSIA
Three Women

PEGGY GUGGENHEIM COLLECTION, VENICE, ITALY
Bathers with a Toy Boat

INDEX